COPING WITH ANXIETY IN AN AGE OF TERRORISM

**Other titles from The American Mental Health Foundation
by Raymond B. Flannery Jr., Ph.D., FAPM**

Becoming Stress-resistant through the Project SMART Program

Posttraumatic Stress Disorder: The Victim's Guide to Healing and Recovery

Violence in the Workplace

*The Assaulted Staff Action Program (ASAP):
Coping with the Psychological Aftermath of Violence*

*Violence in America: Coping with Drugs, Distressed Families, Inadequate
Schooling, and Acts of Hate*

Preventing Youth Violence: A Guide for Parents, Teachers, and Counselors

The Violent Person: Professional Risk Management Strategies for Safety and Care

Violence: Why People Do Bad Things, with Strategies to Reduce that Risk

COPING WITH ANXIETY IN AN AGE OF TERRORISM

Raymond B. Flannery Jr., Ph.D., FAPM

2017

AMHF

AMERICAN
MENTAL
HEALTH
FOUNDATION
BOOKS

American Mental Health Foundation Inc
128 Second Place Garden Suite
Brooklyn New York 11231-4102

Printed in the United States of America

americanmentalhealthfoundation.org

Library of Congress Cataloging-in-Publication Data

Names: Flannery, Raymond B., author.
Title: Coping with anxiety in an age of terrorism / Raymond B.
Flannery Jr., Ph.D., FAPM.
Description: Brooklyn, New York : American Mental Health
Foundation Inc., [2017] | Includes bibliographical references.
Identifiers: LCCN 2016039283 (print) | LCCN 2016053292 (ebook) |
ISBN 9781590565605 (pbk.) | ISBN 1590565606 (pbk.) |
ISBN 9781590565612 (ebook) | ISBN 1590565614 (ebook)
Subjects: LCSH: Terrorism. | Terrorism—Psychological aspects. |
Victims of terrorism. | Terrorism—Prevention.
Classification: LCC HV6431 .F595 2017 (print) | LCC HV6431
(ebook) | DDC 363.32501/9—dc23
LC record available at https://lccn.loc.gov/2016039283

For victims of terrorism worldwide

Contents

Publisher's Foreword

As this book is issued, The American Mental Health Foundation reaches upward and grows toward 100 years of research and philanthropic work. AMHF is dedicated to the welfare of people suffering from emotional problems, with a particular concern for at-risk youth, individuals of any age with special needs, and elders. Historically, AMHF devoted its efforts to bettering quality of treatment, and developing more effective methods, making both available and accessible to individuals of modest incomes. Today, the mission of AMHF lies in three areas: research, publishing, and educational seminars/Webinars.

Coping with Anxiety in an Age of Terrorism extends the mission of this foundation, as well as Dr. Flannery's work, by probing a tragically informing reality of our times: psychological stress brought on by random, mass acts of hatred. As W. H. Auden characterized a different era "The Age of Anxiety," so ours is "The Age of Terrorism." The world appears unduly violent and unpredictable in an unprecedented way. Signs throughout urban-transit systems advise and warn: "if you see something, say something." These signs are in several languages. Paradoxically, there is as yet no profile of a terrorist.

This book is directed toward two audiences: an uneasy, hyper-vigilant public that ever anticipates the random next terrorist incident and professionals toward whom the public turns for support during such events. As Dr. Flannery notes, this book is written to enhance our understanding of terrorism by examining what it actually is and how to cope with the stress that it brings.

Dr. Flannery is a lucid, jargon-free author. He has a sobering yet reassuring message. His body of written work, including 9 books—all available from AMHF— informs over 45 years of dedicated research, clinical treatment, and providing the public with an understanding of violent behavior, and one of its most notorious effects: PTSD and how to cope with each.

* * *

Since inception in the 1920s as one of the pioneering nonprofit foundations of its kind, The American Mental Health Foundation has been a force in research and advocacy. Its major therapeutic advances and improved training methods are described in several publications: the three-part series The Search for the Future. Two of these books are available on the AMHF Web site under the titles *The Challenge for Group Psychotherapy* (volume 1) and *The Challenge for Psychoanalysis and Psychotherapy: Solutions for the Future* (volume 2). Portions of these books are also reprinted on the AMHF Web site in French and German. Volume 3, originally issued at the turn of the millennium, is available from AMHF Books in traditional and e-book formats: *Crucial Choices—Crucial Changes: The Resurrection of Psychotherapy.*

In addition to *Crucial Choices—Crucial Changes* and related books available free on the Web site, the publishing program of AMHF includes (as noted) Dr. Flannery; four classic books (two reissued, two posthumously published) by Erich Fromm; four by Dr. Henry Kellerman on group psychotherapy as well as personality formation and the elusive qualities of delusion; one on the specific psychological stresses faced by women executives, written by Drs. Joanne H. Gavin, James Campbell Quick, and David J. Gavin; and, collaborating with Astor Services for Children & Families, *Early Identification, Palliative Care, and Prevention of Psychotic Disorders in Children and Youth,* the culmination of a two-year study in 2016.

* * *

The costs of promoting research, organizing seminars and Webinars, and disseminating the findings in fulfillment of the mission of AMHF, are high. All gifts, made via PayPal on the foundation Web site or posted to the address listed on the copyright page of this book, constitute a meaningful contribution to the public good. If your commitment is deeper, consider partnering with AMHF in the form of a legacy bequest, so that the foundation would continue to serve society for another 100 years. We thank you for your interest in the urgent subject of the present book and for helping AMHF build a more compassionate society. Please discover the work of The American Mental Health Foundation in greater detail:

americanmentalhealthfoundation.org

Preface

Dateline: Paris, France, November 13, 2015

Thank God it was Friday, even if Friday the Thirteenth. It had been a busy week at the hospital. There had been several emergency, urgent, and routine patient visits nearby Hôpital Saint-Louis. Some of its medical staff had come to relax at Le Carillon, a café and bar, in the city-center near other popular nightlife spots. The café's old sofas and low lighting were familiar friends. Several dozen people walked the streets and vehicle street traffic moved along, until a nondescript black car pulled up in front.

Out stepped a terrorist. Armed with a Kalashnikov, he slipped into Le Carillon and started shooting customers at random. Patrons, including the medical staff, ducked under tables for cover. The terrorist then walked across the street and again started randomly shooting patrons in a second restaurant, Petit Cambodge. It was over in fewer than three minutes. The medical staff worked feverishly to save those whom they could.

These restaurant attacks were part of a larger six-pronged terrorist assault on Paris that ultimately left 130 innocent civilians and 7 terrorists dead, and 368 wounded, many severely. It was a night of multiple targets, indiscriminate shooting, and improvised explosive devices: truly a night of horror. The medical staff could attest to that.

Darkness had descended on the City of Light.

Parisians were severely frightened—terrified actually—the exact outcome the terrorists had coldly planned in attacking innocent civilians. Parisians should have been frightened in the face of death and senseless destruction. This wave of intense fear has also been true for any nation that has been subjected to terrorist incidents.

Who would do such things? Are they insane? Are they evil? Senseless death and destruction seem irrational by any standard. Citizen–victims worldwide struggle to understand what terrorism is and how to protect one's self and one's loved ones.

Terrorist violence is a complicated topic, and there are many fine books on it. However, they are written largely for the academic community and the variety of government agencies charged with protecting us. To date, there has been no concise overview of this subject for the general reader, the average citizen who wants to understand terrorism and how to manage and cope with the anxiety it instills.

This book addresses that need.

We should feel terrified in the face of imminent death and annihilation. It is Nature's biological and psychological way of making us pay attention to a life-threatening situation and to seek safety instantly. However, when the immediate danger has passed, we need to make our understandable anxiety more tolerable, so that we can get on with life without being unduly incapacitated. The tools to manage this anxiety are called *risk management strategies* and they are helpful in coping with the original terrorist incident as well as any subsequent fallout.

This book answers the four basic questions, which are most often posed by terrorist victims: What is terrorism? Who does this? What happens to the victims? and What are the risk management strategies to cope with the original incident and to manage understandable anxiety going forward? This book is written concisely so that we are not overwhelmed by the complexity of terrorism but remain able to use this knowledge to implement the basic risk management strategies to lead reasonably safe and productive lives for ourselves and our loved ones. Since we are likely to experience more terrorist events worldwide in the coming years, mastering the risk management strategies in this book is important for all of us. My hope is that this concise, nontechnical book for average, time-pressed citizens will prove to reduce unnecessary terrorist-related anxieties and ensure good physical and mental health going forward.

We turn first to the basics of terrorism as we begin our journey into the heart of darkness.

* * *

Every author is indebted to a variety of sources that contribute to the work in some helpful way. I am indebted to the academic community of medical and behavioral-sciences researchers, which is continuously expanding our awareness of terrorism to improve risk management strategies to enhance our safety, and to the military and first-responder communities that ensure this safety. I am grateful to the patients who have taught me much about the impact of violence on its victims. I am appreciative of Evander Lomke, president of The American Mental Health Foundation, for supporting my work as part of the foundation mission to enlighten the public and contribute to public welfare on a variety of mental-health issues. Lastly, I am thankful for my wife, Georgina, who sustains my work.

—Raymond B. Flannery Jr., Ph.D., FAPM
Autumn 2016

Author's Note and Editorial Method

Forms of inquiry into the causes, treatment, and risk reduction strategies are constantly being upgraded and the latest research findings should be considered. The present chapters are updated as of autumn, 2016. General guidelines and principles are presented here but, since violence cannot be predicted with one-hundred percent accuracy, this book is not intended as a substitute for the advice and counsel of policing personnel, lawyers, and/or professional counselors who may be necessary in specific situations. Raise any questions that you have with these various professionals, and always weigh and follow their advice first.

With respect to psychological trauma and PTSD, medicines and other forms of treatment are also constantly being upgraded and improved. This book is not intended to provide therapy and is not a substitute for the advice of your physician or professional counselor. Raise any questions that you may have with them and always follow the advice of your physician or counselor. *First.*

* * *

The risk management strategies outlined in this book include both governmental strategies to protect all of us as well as individual stress management approaches that we can each utilize to cope with the anxiety of living in an age of terrorism. One of these strategies involves aerobic exercise. Everyone is advised to begin with a physical exam to be sure that your anxiety is not related to some other medical illness and to have medical clearance for any aerobic exercise that you may want to include. Again, raise any questions that you may have with your physician and always follow the advice of your physician first.

* * *

All of the examples in this book are based on real events that have impacted individuals. In some cases the examples are those of one person, in others they are based on composites of impacted individuals. To the extent possible, identifying information has been omitted to preserve anonymity.

* * *

A listing of References and Select Readings has been provided at the end of the book for further study as well as for all citations.

PART 1

TERRORISM: BASIC CONCEPTS

PART 1

Terrorism: Basic Concepts

We penetrate deeper and deeper into the heart of darkness.
—JOSEPH CONRAD

You cannot shake hands with a clenched fist.
—INDIRA GANDHI

Dateline: Brussels, Belgium, March 22, 2016
Alarm bells rang and sleepy residents in Brussels began the routine motions of yet another routine day. Several began their morning with sweets: beignets, sweet rolls, and similar assorted pastries. Then it was on to the day's activities. Some to town. Some to the airport. Some by car. Some by Metro.

Those who went to the airport were working their way through the departure hall. At 7:48 A.M., it happened. A loud explosion, flames, a powerful percussive blast. Nine seconds later a second explosion similar to the first. Walls, glass, furniture, people: shattered. Some were thrown into the air by the blast. Other victims ran past the wounded on the floor who were no longer able to run. Death, injury, blood, a blanket of dust covered those who had fallen.

Emergency services responded quickly. Priority was given to the most grievously wounded who might survive. Resources were limited. Some of the wounded had to be removed on luggage carts.

> *The agony of the suffering was profound and deeply painful. As the ISIS assailants had hoped, terror filled the air.*

Dateline: Deir ez-Zor, Eastern Syria, March 23, 2016
Alarm bells rang. Sleepy resident began their day here as well. ISIS began the day by handing out sweets to children to celebrate the joy of attacking the Crusaders in Belgium.
> *Thou shalt not kill held little credence here.*

Murdering innocent civilians is the hallmark of terrorists. This slaughter and carnage is as old as human history, with the earliest recorded being terrorist attacks by Zealots against the Romans. This killing of innocents has not changed over the centuries. What has changed is the lethality of the means that are now employed.

In today's age we hear of terrorist events through the various forms of media. They report the most gruesome facts for shock value to draw in their audience. However, this constant drumbeat of violence and mayhem can result in anxiety and a general state of unease in average citizens. Even though the likelihood of being killed in a car accident or being struck by lightning is much more likely than being involved in a terrorist incident, we carry on each day without being unduly anxious or worried about these possible painful outcomes. Our life experiences and those of others provide an understanding of the risks and ways to reduce these risks. This in turn reduces unnecessary worry and anxiety. However, the frequency of terrorist events with their carnage and mayhem may result in understandable civilian anxiety, as many of us do not understand terrorism and what can be done to reduce its risk.

We find ourselves frequently worrying about our own safety, the safety of our loved ones, where we can travel safely, and the like. "Where and when will it end?" is a common refrain.

Terrorism is not going to stop in the short term. It is more a generational issue and we need to adjust to its sporadic outbursts so that we can lead reasonably normal lives during our time on earth. The basic processes that help us to control undue anxiety over car accidents and lighting strikes are the same processes that we can use to keep undue worry about terrorism from ruining our days. Understanding what terrorism is, what the risk management strategies that our governments can employ, and how we as individual citizens are able to cope can reduce anxiety immeasurably. We are not helpless in the face of terrorist events.

This book has four parts. The first part enhances our understanding of terrorism by examining what it actually is. The second part explores the assailants who do these things and the motivations that impel them to commit such heinous acts. Part three next explores the impact of these terrorist events on victims and the treatments available to overcome the psychological trauma and posttraumatic stress disorder (PTSD) that is found in some (but not all) victims, so that these victims can restore a normal sense of daily life. Finally, the last part of the book spells out important risk management strategies based on our understanding of terrorism from the previous three parts. No one to date can predict violence with one-hundred percent accuracy, but these risk management strategies provide us with important tools to reasonably control our lives and to maintain some sense of perspective and contentment.

The one basic principle in all of the great religions and ethical codes of humanity is that we should love one another. We turn now to terrorism and journey deeper and deeper into the heart of darkness, where loving one another has failed.

Terrorism

A large part of why we find it hard to understand terrorism is that there are so many definitions put forth by academicians, researchers, politicians, military personnel, and governmental policy makers. It is not uncommon to hear of religious terrorists, political terrorists, economic terrorists, and the like.

It needn't be this confusing. We need to remember that each terrorist group has a cause that it wants to further but that they all employ a common battle strategy. Instead of fielding a conventional army or dropping bombs, they employ the military strategy of terrorism (Carr, 2002). Terrorism is a military *strategy* that seeks to instill intense fear in a civilian population by committing atrocious, horrifying acts of violence so that the civilian population of the enemy abandons its leaders and policies, and accepts the enemy's demands. Terrorism is not an ideology such as liberalism, conservatism, or socialism. It is a military strategy to force the civilian population to capitulate.

As we shall see in greater detail in the next part, the roots of these various terrorist causes may be found in people who are affluent, people who are highly educated, as well as people who are poor, who have no voice in politics, who are victims of rapid modernization, who are despised for their religious beliefs, and so forth. However, it is also important to note in each of these causes normal caring attachments to other humans who are not similarly impacted, have been truncated and destroyed. Once these attachments have been ruptured, it is easier to kill those perceived as irresponsible. Terrorists obviously have attachments to other members of their groups and we shall examine this paradox in the next part.

Terrorist Group Structure

To attain the goal of frightening any given civilian population into repudiating its leaders, terrorist groups usually have a common structure to attain their goals. Lone wolves, individuals who act alone in the name of the cause but have no direct affiliation with the leaders of the cause, are not part of the group structure and will be discussed separately in the next part on assailants.

A terrorist group has four distinct components. First are the senior leaders of the movement who set out its values and the general warfare strategies to be pursued. Their goals are supported by the second component, the cadre of followers who commit the actual terrorist events. The third component provides the necessary intelligence to engage in these terrorist acts successfully. The fourth component usually works behind the scenes and provides the necessary monies and materials for the successful completion of any given terrorist mission. Nothing is left to chance. Each of the four groupings of members believes in the cause and is willing to engage in violence to attain its end. The leaders and the foot soldiers are also motivated by additional individual reasons to engage in violence, as we shall see in the next part.

Terrorist Weaponry

The strategies and tactics chosen by terrorists vary by the cause but most include the weaponry noted in Table 1. These weapons are divided into two categories:

Table 1. Common Terrorist Weaponry

Conventional Weapons of Destruction
Murders/Beheadings/Stabbings/Drownings/Immolations
Improvised Explosive Devices
Suicide Bombers/Drive-by Shootings
Car Bombs
Bombs/Mortars/Rockets/Missiles
Hijackings
Arson
Rape/Torture/Assaults

Weapons of Mass Destruction
Biological
Chemical
Nuclear
Cyberterrorism

---

conventional weapons of destruction and weapons of mass destruction.

Conventional weapons include a variety of tactics to kill others. Included here would be assignations, beheadings, fatal stabbings, drowning people alive, and burning others to death. Various forms of improvised explosive devices (IED) can be employed in car bombs, suicide bombings, and other forms of drive-by shootings or as timed hidden explosives on planes, buses, and similar settings.

Terrorists also employ some of the weapons found in conventional warfare, such as bombs, mortars, rockets, and launched missiles. Other strategies can include hijackings, arson, torture, assaults, and rapes to humiliate the enemy's females and to implant the assailants' biological roots in the enemy. In recent times, various types of media have been used to deliver frightening messages and threats of death.

As bad as these weapons are, weapons of mass destruction (WMD) pose an even greater threat (Forest, 2015). Biological agents could include bacteria; viruses; and toxins such as smallpox, bubonic plague, anthrax, and similar illnesses. These agents could be used to attack agriculture or the water supply, wherein these germs would spread quickly and harm large numbers of citizens.

Chemical terrorism could include agents such as mustard gas, sarin, ricin and various nerve agents like Saarinen. These agents could be spread in crowds to be maximally effective, and could be delivered by mortars, rockets, or other devices to release these various gases.

Nuclear (radioactive) terrorism could be used to slaughter thousands of people in one attack. People often use the words "a dirty bomb." This refers to a container that has radioactive materials in it so that, when it explodes, citizens would be killed by the blast, have burned skin, and crush injuries, as well as exposure to the cancer carcinogens that are released. Citizens die immediately or over time due to cancer illnesses. Jobs are lost because the land is contaminated for years. Death is present everywhere: in the deceased, in the dying, in those with birth defects, in the land that is dead, and in the minds of those who survive as they contemplate the ubiquitous presence of death at every turn.

Our own age has given rise to cyberterrorism, wherein enemy hackers can steal money from banks online, can disrupt basic daily services such as lighting, water resources, and engage in intelligence gathering among other evils. Banks, power plants (including nuclear power plants), air-traffic control systems, stock exchanges can all be disrupted or totally brought to a standstill. See Laquer (1999) for a thorough analysis of WMD.

As horrific as the use of any of these weapons are, terrorist groups will employ them to bring attention to their causes, especially if these tactics have any chance of being successful in getting the citizens of the enemy to capitulate.

Terrorist Funding Resources

As one might expect, supporting a large group of terrorists in the field is a complicated and expensive proposition. Not only is there a need to buy armaments, but there is the feeding, clothing, provision of transportation, and salaries for terrorist members. The terrorist accountant cannot go to a legitimate bank for a loan and credit cards would not work either. However, large sums of money need to be generated on an ongoing basis, so the terrorist group turns to crime. Table 2 presents some of the more frequent and illegal ways to raise monies.

Table 2. Terrorist Funding Sources

Robbery/Fraud/Forgery
Extortion/Taxation
Kidnapping Ransoms
Protection Money
Smuggling/Piracy
Drugs/Prostitution

Legitimate Businesses
Asset Transfers
Sovereign State Support

The first part of the list outlines the more commonly known methods to raise money illegally. These include various forms of robbery. Fraud and forgery are commonly used methods as are extorting money from civilians from behind the enemy's own lines. Smuggling, piracy, and kidnapping for ransoms are additional forms of robbery. Prostitution, gun-running, and illegal-drug distribution are also common methods to raise money.

At the bottom of Table 2 are more seemingly legitimate ways of raising funds. Some terrorist groups run legitimate businesses such as farms and construction firms, and use the profits to finance slaughter. Transferring assets at gunpoint is a second way of raising resources from legitimate businesses. They transfer assets such as property, inventory, or stock. The terrorists then sell these goods and use the profits to support the terrorist cause.

The governments in some countries have large so-called discretionary funds of money, which can be put to any use. Citizens generally have no voice in how these monies are distributed. Some countries bent on power and influence provide funding to terrorist causes or countries harboring terrorists, so that these sovereign state funds, as they are known, can be used to support terrorist activities in neighboring states.

Stages of Terrorist Attacks

Given that the structure of the terrorist group is intact, given access to the weaponry of destruction, and given the monies to support terrorist activities, terrorist groups plan their attacks on the enemy in stages. Again, nothing is left to chance. Sometimes these events include major venues like the bombing of the World Trade Center; sometimes they are more circumscribed-discrete events like the beheadings of innocent civilians. Both types of events are also planned to maximize possible media coverage. All incidents are meant to maximize fear.

Table 3 outlines the cycle or stages of terrorist events as noted by Horgan (2014). This outline is simplified and easy to remember. This is important as the stages of a terrorist incident are the same stages that the victims' country employs as it plans and executes counterinsurgency incidents. We shall return to Table 3 in part 4, when we study ways to manage anxiety secondary to terrorist events.

In the case of the terrorists, the cycle begins with the decision to attack. The enemy's potential weak spots are considered, and

---

Table 3. Stages of a Terrorist Incident

---

1. Decision to Attack
2. Pre-event Planning Activity
3. Event Execution
4. Post-event Analysis

---

research activity can include visiting and photographing potential sites. Often, possible weaknesses are tested by attacking small targets to gauge what amount of resistance might be provoked. Targets are considered separately and then the target, which is both the easiest to penetrate and where maximum lethality and fear would be greatest, is selected.

The second step is very detailed event planning. This includes both strategic and tactical strategies. Money to finance the event; all forms of intelligence such as the best time of day to strike, the entry point of least resistance, and the best exit strategy; device-testing of explosives, selecting and training the best recruits to commit the act, and planning the logistics of how to send and retrieve the deployed recruits are all carefully considered.

The third step is the execution of the targeted event. These events are staged to create the greatest amount of sudden onset, extensive carnage and property destruction, and quick exit to minimize terrorist losses.

The fourth and final step is a post-incident analysis of how successful the carnage and mayhem inflicted on the enemy actually was; what, if anything, they learned about the enemy's strengths and resilience; and, lastly, how they can improve their lethal approaches for the next enemy encounter.

Although terrorism has been around since at least the first century C.E., some researchers believe that it has been increasing in recent years (e.g., Dutton, 2002) and there are in fact some global changes that may be augmenting the number of angry people who then create angry terrorist groups.

First is the emergence of the global economy. This is increasing the disparity of incomes between peoples, a fact that stirs resentment. The global economy is based on a set of values that emphasize individual over family initiative, material gain, and intense competition. Not all cultures adhere to these values and resent the potential dominance of them. Terrorists exploit that. Second is the urbanization of the global population, as individuals seek better opportunities for themselves and their children. Rapid social change occurs faster in cities and leaves the newcomers anxious and bewildered. Many do not know their way around in the new setting, and most do not know their rights. Terrorists sense this vulnerability and realize that, if they control the cities, they control any given country. A third possible factor is the growth of the worldwide media, especially the twenty-four-hour news outlets. The media provide instant coverage of terrorist events and provides free propaganda and advertising for the terrorist cause. Onsite live coverage of the worst of the carnage serves to maximize fear and often discourages the enemy's civilian population. Terrorists also use the internet to recruit members and to spread the message of their causes with their own media productions.

What Terrorism Is Not

It is important to remember that not all conflicts are terrorist events. Conventional warfare, guerilla warfare, and common criminal behavior are distinct entities that require distinctly different approaches toward their resolution.

Conventional warfare. In conventional wars, armed soldiers in the uniforms of one side attack other armed soldiers in uniforms of the other side. Civilians are not targets. In conventional wars, there are distinct opponents, strategic goals, and the possibility of victory or failure.

In addition, many countries adhere to the United Nations concept of a Just War. A Just War is fought only for the highest of moral purposes. Force is utilized only after all reasonable efforts have been expended to resolve the matter through diplomacy. When force is utilized, only the amount of force that is necessary to resolve the conflict is activated. Steps need to be in place to protect innocent civilians, and all prisoners of war are to be treated humanely. Reprisals against civilians or prisoners of war are outlawed.

Guerilla warfare. Guerillas are groups of armed individuals who attack enemy military forces for power or material goods. They seize and hold civilians, property, and/or territory, and they exercise governance over captured territory and its residents. They do not adhere to the principles of the Just War outlined above, and they do not wear uniforms.

Common criminal behavior. Criminals are not religious, altruistic, or political crusaders. They are primarily concerned with acquiring power to obtain money and material goods. They are often selfish and seek no effects beyond their immediate criminal activities. Innocent civilians are involved only to the extent that the criminal activity somehow directly includes the civilian in the commission of the criminal act.

Research Note

This book is for the reader who is not likely involved in terrorism research. I have distilled the latest findings and present them in nontechnical language. However, the general reader should feel secure in knowing that there is a large body of academicians, researchers, military, and governmental-agency personnel working intensely around the clock to improve our understanding of terrorist enemies and the most beneficial strategies to defeat them.

* * *

This chapter has been written to enhance our understanding of terrorism as a first step in reducing unnecessary anxiety. If we know our enemy and their strategies, we know how to defeat that enemy and enhance our own safety and well-being. The important points to draw from this short review are:

1. *Each* terrorist group has its own individual cause.
2. *All* terrorist groups employ the military strategy called terrorism, which is an attack on innocent civilians to create intense fear.

3. *All* terrorist groups have the same basic structure, access to the same weapons of destruction, and the needed necessary financial resources.

4. *All* terrorist incidents occur in a four-step cycle, the same four-step cycle that can be used to defeat them.

We turn now to enhancing further our understanding of terrorist events by examining in detail the very assailants who commit these horrendous acts.

PART 2

TERRORISM:
THE ASSAILANTS

PART 2

Terrorism: The Assailants

An eye for an eye leaves the whole world blind.
—Mohandas K. Gandhi

The most powerful motive is striving for attachment.
People will kill for it.
—Ernest Becker

Dateline: Chibok, Borno State, Nigeria, April 14–15, 2014
She passed the test. She was now able to murder, permanently disable, maim bodies, and cut throats, and now for the final test. She was strapped with explosives to become a suicide bomber. She awaited her orders.

It had not begun this way. She hated tests and would much rather think about family, friends, boys, and parties. Yet here she was with 269 other girls studying for their final exams in physics at the government secondary school. Suddenly, the school was surrounded by heavily armed militiamen pretending to be guards. They told the girls to follow them, herded them onto trucks, and drove into the mountainous woods to their camps. The girls were frightened, afraid of being killed. Their captors

were the armed militia of Boko Haram, which most often trans-
lates as "Western Education Is Forbidden."

This kidnappng was most likely revenge for an earlier board-
ing-school attack in Yobo in March. All of the 28 male students
at the school were killed. The girls were spared and ordered to go
home and get married. Boko Haram felt its order had been dis-
missed and was now taking revenge at this government school.

After the capture, the Chibok girls were sold as wives or sex
slaves. Most were raped. Some became cooks. None was returned
to a classroom. Boko Haram brainwashed still others to commit
murder, to cut the throats of the enemy, and to blow themselves
up as suicide bombers. No one called it schooling.

Who would commit such acts as murder, maiming of others, and suicide? Who would teach such acts to children? Are these people insane? Are they psychopaths? Are they evil? Could anyone become a cold-blooded killer of hundreds of innocent civilians? What would motivate anyone to do these horrendous acts? What could be the source of such rage?

We focus here on the people who commit terrorist acts. Much of the published literature on terrorism concerns itself with the broad political, economic, and social issues that motivate people to become terrorists and we will examine these. However, people also join the same cause for a variety of other reasons that reflect common criminal and violent attitudes. The terrorist literature is mostly silent on these ciminal matters, silent as well on a second important aspect: that of caring attachments. Your caring attachments, your friends, in part shape who you are and what you become. The same is true for terrorists. Thus, in addition to the main group causes for terrorist behavior, we shall also include the role of individual motivations for violence and the important role of caring attachments in these processes.

We begin, however, with the basic domains of good physical and mental health in average citizens. As we shall see, these domains become disrupted in assailants and victims. In assailants, these domains lead to violent extremism; in victims, for different reasons, they impair recovery.

The Domains of Good Physical and Mental Health

The domains for good health are three: reasonable mastery, the ability to shape the environment to meet one's needs; caring attachments to others; and a meaningful prosocial purpose in life to motivate engagement with the world in constructive ways each day.

Reasonable Mastery. Reasonable mastery refers to the ability to shape our environments to meet our needs. We have to acquire the necessary cognitive, behavioral, and emotional skills to be productive citizens in our work and personal lives. We acquire an education, the basic social skills necessary to relate with others, and the ability to express our feelings tactfully. With these skills, we earn a living, interact with others in the community, and have the resources to care for ourselves and our families, as well as to pursue our goals in life. We have shaped the environment to meet our needs.

Reasonable mastery is divided into three basic types. The first is self-care and refers to having the ability to manage diet, exercise, finances, time, life stress, and the ability to self-soothe ourselves in the face of life's inevitable down periods. The second set of mastery skills refers to interpersonal skills. Included here are empathy for others, sharing, verbal conflict-resolution skills, and generally cooperative group-interaction skills. The third set of skills is academic and refers to mastering the basic knowledge of the culture, to learning a trade or having a professional career, and to mastering computers and the media in general.

Good problem solvers have a basic problem-solving approach that is effective in this regard. First, they correctly identify the problem to be solved. If they are angry at work, they do not express the anger at home: They solve the problem at work. Second, they gather information to solve the problem. They draw on past experience, seek the suggestions of others, and/or read books or articles on the topic. Next, they devise a series of thoughtful strategies to solve the problem at hand. They develop more than one strategy in case the first solution does not work. Finally, they implement the proposed solution and check to see if it has worked.

Adaptive problem solvers know something else as well. They know that at times they will not have the needed resources to solve a given problem or even that some problems cannot be solved. In these cases, they stop trying. Reasonable mastery also includes knowing when to stop wasting time and energy.

Poor problem solving may result in not meeting one's goals, medical or psychiatric illness, financial shortfalls, feeling overwhelmed, and being unable to think clearly.

Caring Attachments. Caring attachments are the meaningful bonds or links that we have with other humans. Humans are social animals and being close to others make us feel good. The absence of caring others in our lives leads to a painful loneliness.

The impetus to study caring attachments arose during and after World War II. The war had disrupted families through death, abandonment, and relocation. There were also several orphans. Psychiatrist René Spitz (Lynch, 1977) was among the first to call attention to this human need for attachments and how its absence could be deadly. In 1945–46, he studied ninety-one infants in orphanages. All of them were well cared for but thirty-four died in the last three months of their first year in spite of good care and no obvious medical illnesses.

John Bowlby (1982), a British physician, was also studying this parent child interaction. A parent literally gives life to the baby at birth certainly, but also in the baby's early years, when the infant is unable to feed, clothe, shelter, and protect herself or himself. Bowlby noticed an important pattern. When the mother was with the child, the baby was happy. However, if the mother was drawn away, the baby would scream in protest until the mother returned. When the mother returned, the baby would again become quiet but, if the mother did not return, the baby would become despondent and depressed. The child remained withdrawn from others, as if not wanting to be abandoned again.

This early work teaches the importance of caring attachments for sustaining life and making human beings reasonably content. Subsequent research on adults has further clarified the importance of human attachments. There are several psychological benefits that accrue and these include companionship, emotional support in good times and difficult periods, information about problem-solving life's stressful problems, and instrumental factors in the forms of lending money or political favors. Similarly, we now know that certain types of relationships are harmful. These include relationships marked by physical/sexual/verbally abusive interactions, emotional over involvement in the lives of others, emotional demandingness, and interpersonal skill deficiency.

In addition to the psychological benefits, there are physiological benefits as well. Physiologist James Lynch (1977) noted early on that in caring relationships a person's cardiovascular system (blood pressure and pulse), the individual's immune system to fight off upper respiratory infections, and a person's endorphin opioid system (endorphins are chemicals in the brain that make us feel good) were all strengthened in the presence of caring attachments; the reverse was true in socially isolated individuals. He also found that the absence of caring attachments resulted in premature death (Lynch, 2000).

One important aspect of caring attachments is the component of empathy. Empathy refers to our ability to understand the feeling states of others, since we have experienced the same feelings in similar situations. We can understand the sadness and depression of someone who has recently lost a loved one since we all have had similar experiences. Empathy plays an important role in understanding violence. Empathy forms the basis for moral development and the need to express concern for the welfare of all. Disruptions in empathy may produce disruptions in moral development that limit the capacity to appreciate the suffering being visited upon another through violent behavior.

Meaningful Purpose in Life. All of us need a reason to get up in the morning and invest our energy in the world. This is called a meaningful, prosocial purpose in life that motivates us to be contributing members of society. We develop a sense of coherency about our lives. This sense of a coherent, meaningful purpose in life is composed of three parts. Our meaningful purpose needs to provide a sense of world manageability, world comprehensibility, and a purpose for investing our energy in the world each day (Antonosky, 1979). Our sense of coherence helps us to establish some specific task in life such as careers, rearing our children, participating in some important community activity. The meaningful purpose helps us to keep life in perspective and to buffer the life stressors that come our way.

Human beings are part biological (the body) and part psychological (the mind). The mind knows that at some point the body will die and it is human nature to find a way to live on in the minds of others after one's death. The goals that society, often values, such as power, money, and fame end at death. However, the most robust meaningful prosocial purposes in life involve being concerned for the lives of others and these need not end at death. Rearing children, creating trusts, creating various works of art, and community social causes are all meaningful purposes for the individuals who espouse them in their own lives when they are alive and are all examples of how to live on in the minds of others after death.

Reasonable mastery, caring attachments to others, and a meaningful purpose in life are the three domains of good physical and mental health that foster normal childhood development and adaptive adult functioning. In violence, these domains are disrupted, negatively modified, or absent. Normal moral growth has not developed.

Understanding Terrorist Violence

Most violence occurs when people are angry. Given the under-standing of normal growth and development, we are now in a bet-ter position to understand why terrorist assailants are angry and kill, maim, destroy property, and commit other horrendous acts. To do this adequately, we need to understand the two potential sources of anger and aggression that we mentioned at the begin-ning of this section. The first is the terrorist group's motivation for its cause. What is the perceived injustice that has led to this ter-rorist mayhem? The second is to understand the various individual reasons for joining the terrorist cause and committing violent acts. While the terrorist usually has both a reason to join the cause and a reason to behave violently as an individual in that group, not everyone joins the same cause for the same individual reason. For example, some may join the same political terrorist group but may do so to gain social acceptance, to rape or murder, to give meaning to their lives, etc. We begin with general, common terrorist causes.

Table 1 presents a list of common terrorist causes that groups of individuals espouse. Political terrorist groups are found through-out the world.

There are terrorists on the Left who want government to provide a more equal distribution of goods and services to all citizens. There are terrorists on the Right who want a limited government so that individual citizens have more freedom to do as they please. There are also anarchist terrorist groups who want no state government at all.

Closely allied to this is state-sponsored terrorism wherein the government of a nation is involved in seeking the destruction and

Table 1. Common Terrorist Causes

Political
  Left
  Right
  Anarchy
State-sponsored
Religious
Ethnonational
Economic
Ideological
  Animal Rights
  Racism
  Ecology

---

downfall of another country for political or economic gain. Some examples: Al-Qaeda in Afghanistan, Shining Path in Peru, Hezbollah in Lebanon.

A second frequent terrorist-motivating cause is that of faith-based religious causes. In these cases, the adherents of one faith seek to convert another faith group to their traditions or to exterminate the other group as being basically evil. Examples here could include ISIS in the Middle East and the World Uyghur Separatists in China.

International terrorists are seeking territorial gains. They are either trying to gain back their own lands previously taken from them or seeking to expand their own borders at the expense of neighboring countries. Examples here could include the Irish Republican Army, the Chechen Rebels, and Hamas in Palestine.

Economic terrorists are usually greedy criminals seeking to gain as much fortune as they can at the expense of citizens of a country. They exploit governmental and/or policy weaknesses for their personal gain. An example here is the Farc guerillas in Colombia.

Lastly, there are ideological causes, wherein a group of people form a cause on a specific topic, such as animal rights, racism in various forms, and ecological matters.

These common group social causes often have their roots in societies wherein there are violations of basic human rights, economic deprivation, great disparity between poor and rich, no democratic voice in governance, despotism, a failed or weak state, no rule of law, corrupting and/or rapid modernization. If these grievances anger individuals over long enough period of time, terrorism may emerge as an attempt to change the status quo to a more favorable balance.

Individual Causes of Violence

As we noted earlier, people also join the terrorist causes for their own personal reasons. We next explore the large body of data on the reasons individuals become violent. They are grouped in four theories: cultural, biological, sociological, and psychological and are outlined in Table 2. See Flannery (2009, 2016) for more detailed presentations.

Cultural Theory. The culture may be defined as the customary beliefs, social forms, and material traits of a people. There are several cultural theories but the one that best explains the outbreak of violence is the theory of *anomie* by Émile Durkheim (1997). In this theory, the five basic institutions of any society—govern-

Table 2. Theories of Human Violence

Cultural   Anomie

Biological   Genetics
                     Cortex/Limbic System
                     Medical Illnesses

Sociological   Poverty
                     Inadequate Schooling
                     Discrimination
                     Domestic Violence
                     Substance Abuse
                     Easily Available Weapons
                     The Media

Psychological   Mastery
                         Personal Self-care Skills
                         Interpersonal Skills
                         Academic Skills
                     Motivation

ment, business, families, schools, religion—put forth the rules that that society's citizens are to live by and to rear their children accordingly. When these basic rules are humane and effective, that society has a sense of what prosocial behavior is expected and a sense of community is established.

However, when there is a major shift in a culture, these five institutions are thrown into turmoil, the rules for behavior become disrupted, and the sense of community cohesion is lost. Our current culture is undergoing such a transformation or paradigm shift with the advent of the computer and rapid modernization. The new rules for behavior are evolving and the traditional value system of hard work, self-denial, and concern for the welfare of others has been challenged by a competing values' system of me first, material goods, and instant gratification.

Societies undergoing these cultural upheavals have more mental illness, more substance abuse, more suicide, and more violence. This cultural theory disrupts all three of the domains of good health. It is hard to master a constantly changing world, there is a less cohesive sense of caring attachments, and a meaningful prosocial purpose in life constantly needs to be rethought.

Biological Theories. Although many of us think that the agents of these despicable acts must be crazy or have been born this way, there is little evidence to support this in most incidents. It seems reasonable that there must be some genetic basis to violence other than acts of self-protection, but to date there is no consistent evidence of this in general. There is some evidence to support a genetic basis for some mental illnesses in a small fraction of violent episodes.

We do know that injuries to the cortex and the limbic system—where feelings are registered in the brain—can result in violent outbursts. Tumors, head injuries, viruses, birth defects, exposure to lead, and untreated PTSD may result in violence in some as the cortical-control centers of the brain are damaged. In addition, there are certain medical and psychiatric illnesses that contain the potential for violence. Some of the more common ones are delerium, glycemic conditions, lupus, seizures, thyroid conditions, attention deficit/hyperactivity disorder (ADHD), depression, serious mental illness, and substance abuse. Under severe stress, the brain may also revert to old brain stem (OBS) functioning. The OBS is at the back of the head and controls our basic vital life processes. Under severe stress, the cortex, where we normally do our thinking and reasoning, shuts down: the OBS is activated and the individual reacts with "a kill or be killed" mindset.

The biological bases for violent acts are extremely low. Most of these acts are perpetrated by willful, rational people. In the few cases in which biology is at the root of the violence, the domain of reasonable mastery is disrupted.

Sociological Theories. These theories thought to contribute to violence are well known and include poverty, inadequate schooling, discrimination in its various forms, domestic violence, substance abuse, easily available weapons, and violence in the various media formats. Since these factors are covered in detail elsewhere (Flannery, 2006, 2009), they will not be reviewed here.

What is not generally well known is that each sociological factor relates to major defects in caring attachments. For example, poor people have few social supports, students are without enough teachers, those discriminated against or in domestic-violence relationships are in harmful caring attachments, and so forth. In general, the sociological theories reflect disruptions in the domain of caring attachments, and often reflect a lack of empathy as a key component in the commission of angry, violent acts.

Psychological Theories. The psychological theories refer to two components: an individual's coping skills and an individual's motivation for all behaviors, including violence.

An individual's coping skills refer to that person's self-care skills, interpersonal skills, and academic skills, as we have noted above. Deficits in these areas can result in maladaptive problem-solving outcomes that fail both the individual and society. The inability to solve problems in a socially acceptable way can result in increased frustration and anger, especially if the state of frustration is chronic in nature.

In the face of this inability to participate in more socially acceptable ways, many turn to antisocial values. This behavior is motivated by anger, selfishness, self-indulgence, enforcement of one's own sense of justice, and similar self-defeating stances. See Table 3 for some of the more common forms. The psychological theories may disrupt all three of the domains of good health, separately and together.

Table 3. Common Motivational Factors in Violence

Acceptance by Peers
Catharsis of Anger
Despair
Dominance of Others
Enforcement of Personal Sense of Justice
Excitement
Jealousy
Revenge
Selfishness
Shame
Status

Caring Attachments and Terrorism

Having examined both the broad causes that give rise to terrorist groups as well as the various individual causes for violence, we turn more fully to the question: Why do some people make antisocial choices instead of prosocial choices in making meaning in life? The role of caring attachments in this process is a crucial factor that is often overlooked.

"Normal People"

As we have noted, caring attachments are basic to human survival, growth, and a meaningful purpose in life. Attachments are a biological necessity for survival and all human beings seek them out. When individuals have good caring attachments with meaningful prosocial values, they are productive members of society and make our lives buoyant and enriched. Sadly, we all know of people with caring attachments but also have antisocial meaning in life that result in terrorism and other forms of violence whose purpose is to destroy life.

How did this antisocial mindset emerge? The answer paradoxically is the role of caring attachments in the lives of the assailants. Since terrorists are groups of people and they don't kill each other, there must be some form of bond present and we turn now to what might be some of the components of this bond. We begin with peer pressure.

Given the biological innate nature to reach out to others in attachments, individuals are influenced by the others to whom they reach out and not always with the best of outcomes. Psychologist Stanley Milgram (Horgan, 2014) conducted a famous experiment on obedience to authority as a way of being accepted by others. In his study, two people entered the laboratory. One (a confederate of Dr. Milgram) agreed to receive electric shocks to improve learning. A second naive person was asked to sit at a control board and administer shocks in increasing intensity "to improve" learning. In reality, there was no electric current running to the learner's body. The learner, however, feigned pain when Dr. Milgram told the naive person to increase the shock intensity. Even with the learner feigning great pain and agony, the person administering the shock kept doing as the authority figure requested. Over two-thirds of Dr. Milgram's subjects who thought that they were administering true electric shocks did as they were told in order to be accepted by the authority figure.

Here were good people administering pain to others as a means of social acceptance. They did not view themselves as evil but rather as individuals doing something for science. Good people can do bad things in the interest of caring attachments.

A second way in which the need to develop caring attachments can become disrupted arises when social conditions and basic human needs interact. Another psychologist, Ervin Staub (Denton, 2007) sought to study the development of evil in groups of people. He enumerated several important steps that can impact any one of us to become violent and malicious when faced with frustration over our basic needs (e.g., material deprivation, political chaos, and so forth), the exact issues that we noted above that give rise to various terrorist causes.

The frustrated group with its caring attachments to each other defines its enemy as evil, and accuses that enemy of destructive acts (Denton, 2007). The frustrated group develops a sense of its own just cause as fear and anger toward the enemy group rises. The morally just frustrated group then engages in violent acts against the perceived enemy. This level of violence can include murder, rape, robbery, assault, and terrorist mayhem. The group will continue its violence until the frustrated need has been met and the caring attachments of the group have been preserved.

These examples illustrate how normal people seeking out necessary caring attachments can be influenced in negative ways. This in no way excuses the resultant terrorist and violence events, but it does suggest the importance and power of caring attachments in shaping values and behaviors. People have choices.

Lone Wolves

Lone wolfs are individuals who seek affiliation with various terrorist causes. They are not involved in the development of the terrorist cause, they often are nowhere near the basic site of the terrorist group, and they typically do not know any specific person in the group. They do, however, have some sense of kinship with the cause and the people that it oppresses. Hence, they engage in some terrorist activity on their own in a country or place not considered to be the main location of the terrorist activity. Lone wolves can be motivated by any of the common terrorist causes and by any of the individual theories of violence. However, the question of these individuals is the same question we have asked with respect to terrorist groups: Why do lone wolves choose an antisocial meaning in life? Caring attachments may again help us to understand this phenomenon.

Mother Teresa once noted that loneliness and the feeling of being unwanted is the most terrible poverty. Lone wolves are essentially isolated men and women. They are like islands cut off from others. In addition to having difficulties in developing caring attachments, they also have problems developing a meaningful purpose in life. They are like Eric Hoffer's *True Believers* (Hoffer, 1966). True believers have basically empty lives, and they often join causes to give their lives meaning. They might join political or community causes. This provides the possibility of caring attachments plus a possible, if temporary, meaning to life. However, these individuals never internalize the values or beliefs of the cause. When the cause is over or dies, the true believer's attachments and meanings die as well and the believer drifts on to the next cause. This absence of true caring attachments and the need to feel associated with others may lead some individuals to becoming lone wolves. (See Simon, 2013, for an extended discussion.)

By any standard, the carnage and pain inflicted by terrorists in groups or by lone wolves is unacceptable. This is especially true for the victims of violence to whom we now direct our attention.

PART 3

TERRORISM: THE VICTIMS

PART 3

Terrorism: The Victims

Never shall I forget those moments that murdered my God.
And my soul turned my dreams to dust.

—Elie Weisel

It is such a secret place, the land of tears.

—Antoine de Saint-Exupéry

Dateline: New York, New York, September 11, 2001
Why me? Why me? he asked in an empty room in his office suite
on a top floor. He had called his family and said his good-byes in
case he didn't make it. They were in tears. He was in tears. "Stay
calm," he repeated. "Stay calm." The fire was spreading but he
had choices. He could wait until the fire suffocated or burned
him to death. He could jump out a window and hope that he
had a fatal heart attack on the way down or that he smashed his
skull on the concrete below and died instantly....

He had taken a business administration course in college
and remembered the professor saying that every problem had
a solution.

The "problem" was several floors below his office. At 8:46
A.M. on a late-summer morning, a commercial airliner on a

suicide mission crashed into the North Tower of the World Trade Center. Unused jet fuel spread the flames quickly and was aided by the paper stock of hundreds of printer copies throughout the building. The steel frame of the tower began to buckle. People, who could, ran for their lives.

In the office above, panic had set in. There was no way out. No time for phone calls. No time to devise an escape route. Would he choose to be burned alive or jump to a certain death? He said a final, silent prayer. And then…he jumped into the abyss. Traveling at 150 miles per hour, he was likely conscious when his skull shattered like a dropped egg on the concrete pavement below.

Why me?

Why me? is the universal plea of victims as they try to make sense of what has befallen them in the aftermath of a traumatic event. Without doubt, the World Trade Center (WTC) terrorist event was traumatic, significant in its scope, and painful in its consequences. Research studies and general surveys to assess its impact have focused on differing sets of victims and issues, so that drawing a fully complete analysis of the impact of this event is not easily done.

Taken as a whole, the evidence indicates general agreement that there were nearly 3,000 WTC persons killed and another 6,000 suffered a variety of injuries. Most of the victims were civilians, except for 343 firefighters and 71 law-enforcement officers. Since the target was the WTC, several foreign nationals from 62 countries were included among the fatalities. Great Britain, Canada, the Dominican Republic, India, Japan, and South Korea suffered the most casualties. Many of the injuries resulted in temporary or permanent disability, painful bodily injuries requiring multiple surgeries, and the onset of chronic conditions, such as cancer and respiratory problems. Economically, this incident resulted in the loss of 71,000 jobs and $36 billion worth of labor and capital costs.

The toll on the minds of the survivors was equally widespread. Victims have included the WTC survivors, the first responders, and volunteers who arrived; the volunteers who agreed to clean the debris field; all of the citizens at ground level who watched this unfold and who ran from the toxic fumes when the towers collapsed; the families of the deceased and wounded; and parents and children worldwide, who watched these events unfold on the media. A great many had psychological trauma at the time of the incident and many went on to develop PTSD. Thirty-one days later, the Mailman School of Public Health of Columbia University (Mailman, 2015) issued a report on the WTC registry of survivor-enrollees, finding that 20 percent of its 5,896 enrollees displayed either PTSD or depression and that many had both.

As with the research on physical suffering, there have been many studies of the psychological state of many different types of victims. The general conclusion across these studies is similar to the Mailman (2015) findings. A great many victims had psychological trauma in those first days and a great many went on to develop PTSD. Since many victims sought private therapy or did not seek help at all, the true extent of those with psychological trauma and PTSD will never be known. We know from those who did seek care that the suffering was intense during the first days after the incident and remained disabling for many years later.

Given the extent of this mental suffering of these terrorist victims, let us turn now to a detailed understanding of psychological trauma and PTSD.

Psychological Trauma and PTSD

The American Psychiatric Association in its fifth-edition *Diagnostic and Statistical Manual of Mental Disorders* (2013) considers an individual to have been exposed to a traumatic event when the person experienced, witnessed, or was confronted with an event or events that involved actual or threatened death or serious injury, or a threat to the physical integrity of the self or others. Psychological trauma is a person's physical and psychological response to a potentially life-threatening event that is usually sudden and unexpected and is an event over which the victim has no control, no matter how hard he or she tries.

There are any number of traumatic events that one may encounter. These are basically divided into two groupings: natural disasters and human-perpetrated violence. Natural disasters are frightening and stem from the laws of physics. For example, hurricanes are the way the natural world distributes heat over the surface of the earth to ensure stable environments over time. Victims eventually come to understand these laws of nature and physics and the psychological trauma subsides. However, human-perpetrated violence is more difficult to assimilate psychologically. Evil acts seemingly perpetrated by twisted minds that result in such destruction are harder to comprehend and accept.

Any of us can become victims in at least one of these ways. First, we can become victims by direct act. We are the person who is robbed, raped, mugged, and so forth. Second, we can become victims by witnessing these dreadful events happening to others. Third, we can become victims by being told by victims what has happened to them. This third way is a significant problem for first responders, law enforcement, and health care providers, all of whom must file a report on any incident to which they respond.

Domains and Symptoms

We have noted earlier the domains of good physical and mental health include reasonable mastery to shape the environment to meet our needs, caring attachments to others with their important physical and psychological benefits, and a meaningful prosocial purpose in life. We have seen that these domains are disrupted in terrorist assailants. Sadly, they may also be disrupted in the lives of traumatized victims.

By definition of a terrorist event, the victim has lost mastery as the victim has no control over the event. He or she has no way to shape the terrorist event to preclude a painful outcome.

In addition, terrorist events tear apart caring attachments. Victims correctly perceive that the world is not safe and they withdraw before suffering further harm. However, just at the time victims would benefit from the presence of caring attachments, we nonvictims pull away as well. Violence teaches us how tenuous our links are to Mother Earth. We understand that it could easily have been us, and we physically and psychologically withdraw from the victims. In addition, we blame the victims for what has befallen them. Statements such as, "If you didn't walk across the corner at dusk, you would not have been robbed" or "If you hadn't worn your short shorts, you would not have been raped" blame the victim. Rather than seeing them as victims of crimes that were not their fault, we blame them. For we nonvictims, this creates the illusion that we would not behave so foolishly ourselves and thus would not become victims. However, this illusion is just that: one that can easily be dispelled.

Terrorist events also disrupt our meaningful prosocial purposes in life. The development of these life purposes are based on the assumptions that the world is safe, orderly, and predictable. When violence happens, safety is understandably the primary concern. Victims withdraw to where it is safe. If the world does not seem safe, victims withdraw from the world. Order and predictability are forgone in the interests of safety.

In addition to seeking safety, terrorists have a second impact on the victims' meaningful prosocial values. Prosocial meanings in life for most people concern helping others and contributing in some way to bettering society. Doing useful work, sustaining a marriage, rearing children, and supporting community activities are common examples of meaningful prosocial endeavors, as we have seen. Violence, including terrorist violence, disrupts these meaningful purposes. Safety is the prime concern and being engaged with the world is put on hold. Victims have encountered evil. When safety is assured, victims must address the problem of human-perpetrated evil acts before normal prosocial purposes can be restored.

Victims are good people who try to do their best and would not knowingly harm others deliberately. Thus, they ask themselves the universal questions: Why me? Why us? We are good people. Victims are attempting to restore meaning in their lives. Answering these questions is serious, painful, and difficult to resolve, but for life to return to some sense of normalcy, this issue must be addressed. We will return to the problem of "Why me?" later in this section.

Along with these disrupted domains, trauma victims have symptoms. Every medical condition manifests signs or symptoms that all is not well and psychological trauma is no exception. Psychological trauma and PTSD (which we shall examine shortly) have the same sets of three types of symptoms arranged in four clusters, and these are summarized in Table 1.

Physical Symptoms. The physical symptoms arise from the rush of adrenaline in our bodies when the event occurs. It may result in hypervigilance; exaggerated startle responses; difficulties with sleep, concentration, and memory; as well as mood irritability, especially anger and depression. The end result is fear, anxiety, and great discomfort.

Intrusive Symptoms. As if all this were not enough, victims cannot shake the memories from their minds. They experience recollections of the events during the day, have nightmares and dreams of the events at night, and often experience flashbacks (see below). In addition, "triggers" or symbolic reminders of the event can result in the physical symptoms as well as more intrusive memo-

**Table 1. Symptoms of Psychological Trauma
and Posttraumatic Stress Disorder (PTSD)**

Physical Symptoms	Hypervigilance
	Exaggerated Startle Response
	Difficulty Sleeping
	Difficulty with Concentration, Memory
	Mood Irritability—Especially Anger and Depression
Intrusive Symptoms	Recurring, Distressing Recollections (Thoughts, Memories, Dreams, Nightmares, Flashbacks)
	Physical or Psychological Distress at an Event that Symbolizes the Trauma Grief or Survivor Guilt
Avoidant Symptoms	Avoiding Specific Thoughts, Feelings, Activities, or Situations
	Diminshed Interest in Significant Activities
	Restricted Range of Emotions (Numbness)
	Persistent Negative Cognitions
	Persistant Negative Moods

ries. Victims may also experience grief or survivor guilt. These are also forms of intrusive memories as they keep us attached in memory to those lost.

Avoidant Symptoms. Since the physical and intrusive symptoms are so unpleasant, many victims choose to withdraw from much of ongoing live, which can result in two types or clusters of avoidant symptoms.

The first cluster centers on withdrawal and avoidance. Victims withdraw from the scene of the traumatic incident as much as is possible. This avoids more physical and intrusive symptoms in the short term. Unfortunately, over time this tendency to withdraw generalizes to other aspects of family, work, and community life. Avoidant victims continue to withdraw and restrict their range of felt emotions. They experience a low, but ongoing, dysphoric state.

The second avoidant cluster concerns itself with persistent negative cognitions and moods. Disturbances in cognitions might include amnesia of the event or negative beliefs about the self. (For example, "I am bad." "No one can be trusted." "I am damaged goods.") Similarly, there can be present negative emotional states such as fear, horror, anger, shame, guilt, or anhedonia (the inability to feel pleasure).

The disrupted domains of health and the symptoms associated with trauma produce significant and disabling symptoms. Unfortunately, if not properly treated, they can last until death. Table 2 presents a basic checklist for traumatic disruptions.

Table 2. Disruptions in Psychological Trauma and PTSD

Domains of Good Health		*Symptoms*	
Mastery	[ ]	Physical	[ ]
Attachments	[ ]	Intrusive	[ ]
Meaning	[ ]	Avoidant	[ ]

The Biology of Psychological Trauma

We noted earlier that psychological trauma involves both a psychological as well as physiological response. The biological changes in traumatic events are complex. (See Flannery, 2016c for a more detailed review.) Some of the basic changes are noted here.

First, traumatic events activate the startle response. This is the body's mechanism to keep us alive. We have all had the experience of crossing a street without seeing an oncoming car. The car honks and we jump back on the curb to safety. This is our startle response, which reacts in fractions of a second. It is nature's way to ensure our survival. When the startle response is activated, the adrenal glands release adrenalin. In the body, the adrenalin increases breathing, dilates pupils to see more clearly, increases blood flow to the heart and muscles, releases cortisol to clot blood, and increases sugar into the bloodstream, so that the person has needed energy to fight, faint, or flee. At the same time, adrenalin in the brain causes the person to focus clearly and to rivet attention on the traumatic incident. When the crisis has passed and the victim is coping reasonably well, the body returns to its normal resting state. If the traumatic incident is not addressed, the body will remain highly activated.

A second major biological concern is that of recounting the event to secure help. The ability to tell others how one feels can be compromised in two ways. The first is through Broca's Area shutdown. In the brain, just above the middle of the left eyebrow, is Broca's Area. It permits us to describe to ourselves and others what we are thinking, feeling, and experiencing. Under severe stress, Broca's Area shuts down and the person is literally left speechless. As the stress subsides, the ability to speak returns. The second recounting issue may arise in a part of the brain known as the hippocampus. Feeling states in humans are generated in the brain's limbic system. The limbic system has two major components: the amygdala, which registers all feeling states (anxiety, anger, depression, fear, happiness, and so forth) and the hippocampus, which permits the person to label the emotion and to communicate it to the brain and then to others. In some cases of untreated PTSD, the hippocampus may atrophy or die. The victim can recount thoughts and experiences but not feelings. The good news is that over time the hippocampus regenerates itself and the ability to communicate what one feels returns.

Finally, we want to pay attention to the biological process of *kindling*. When the body is under continuing traumatic stress, the adrenalin that keeps being generated will be absorbed into the limbic system, much the way a dry sponge absorbs water. This extra adrenalin in the limbic system sensitizes the limbic system so that subsequent minor physical events that normally produce adrenalin (such as dancing or riding a bicycle) will produce full traumatic disruptions in the victim, as if the original event were occurring again. This phenomenon is known as kindling and can be frightening to victims who are not aware of this possibility. For example, having intrusive memories when swimming to calm down can be frightening, until the victim understands what is occurring.

The Stages of Trauma

Psychological trauma and PTSD have their own sequence of events or stages if the terrorist or other critical incident is not properly addressed. These stages are outlined in Figure 1.

Figure 1. Stages in Psychological and Posttraumatic Stress Disorder

---

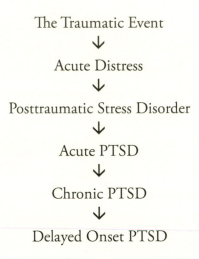

The Traumatic Event
↓
Acute Distress
↓
Posttraumatic Stress Disorder
↓
Acute PTSD
↓
Chronic PTSD
↓
Delayed Onset PTSD

The traumatic event occurs and individuals may become victims of psychological trauma. Any or all of the health domains may be negatively impacted, and these traumatized individuals may also have any or all of the symptoms. The individual's response is key here. Those who seek help and attempt to restore some degree of normality in their daily routines will over time recover. Those who do not seek help or refuse treatment will continue to have problems. Untreated trauma and PTSD last until death.

Victims are given thirty days to restore some degree of normalcy in their lives, given whatever terrorist material destruction or other human-perpetrated event has occurred. This statistic includes victims of both natural disasters and human-perpetrated violence. Victims recover much more quickly from natural disasters than from human-perpetrated violence, which is why the recovery period is thirty days on average.

By medical convention, on the thirty-first day, if the victim continues to experience any of the domain or symptom disruptions noted in Table 2, the victim develops PTSD (disordered functioning resulting in stress after the critical incident has passed). There are three types of PTSD.

The first is acute PTSD. Here, the victim has disrupted health domains and/or PTSD symptoms, and has not sought treatment or been able to recover his or her own. Acute PTSD lasts for three months.

The second is chronic PTSD. If the victim did not seek help in the previous three months, then in month four chronic PTSD is assessed. If the victim continues to avoid treatment, the health domains and symptom disruptions will last until death.

The third type of PTSD is called delayed onset PTSD. In these cases, victims experience the disruptions noted in the thirty-day period of acute stress. The victim seemingly recovers and gets on with his or her life. However at some point after six months of normal living, a trigger or symbolic reminder will occur and the delayed onset victim will again experience the domain and symptom disruptions associated with the original incident. Since all traumatic incidents involve loss, including loss of one's innocence of the world, the trigger or symbolic reminder may be a loss of some form, e.g., the death of a loved one, the loss of property or animals or the loss of one's hearing or vision through normal aging.

The following is an example of delayed onset PTSD. A male teenager was serving Sunday Mass at the local parish church. He came home in a state of severe hypervigilance and preoccupation. He kept his personal distress to himself, told no one what had happened, and got on with his life as best he could. Seven years later, as a young adult, he went to visit his family. The family subscribed to the city newspaper. That day, the paper broke a story on abusive priests with a picture on page one of the various abusers. The son saw the photograph. Included in the photograph was the photograph of the priest who had abused him and he began to experience the psychological trauma symptoms that he had experienced years earlier, when he was abused. The photograph of the priest had served as the trigger. This is an example of not seeking help for terrorist and traumatic events. The disruptions will not go away on their own.

Special Issues

Psychological trauma and PTSD are often accompanied by other complicating factors. The more common ones are noted here.

Dissociation. Dissociation refers to a process in the brain that may occur in traumatic events. When the person is faced with a traumatic, life-threatening event, the startle response is activated and the person focuses on survival. The brain also has the remarkable ability to put unnecessary information out of our immediate attention. This information is stored as a memory trace in the brain. This process of the splitting of information unnecessary for survival and storing it in memory is called dissociation. After the crisis has passed, the stored memories return to the conscious brain suddenly. These experiences are called flashbacks. Flashbacks are most common in combat and rape victims.

Major Depression. Traumatic events are depressing by nature: loss of life, loss of bodily functions, loss of income, loss of property, loss of pets, loss of community. Most commonly, many times there are multiple losses. Over time, the depression may become biologically rooted and greatly impair functioning.

Complicated Grief. Related to major depression is complicated grief. Complicated grief is more intense than normal grieving and includes marked yearning for the lost, social withdrawal, and the loss of meaningful purpose in life.

Generalized Anxiety Disorder. Some victims retain the anxiety first experienced during the traumatic incident. Over time, they begin to worry and fear excessively about many aspects of living.

The Repetition Compulsion. One would think that, if one escaped from the lions' den, one would not return to the lions' den. However, there is a subset of victims that do return to situations similar to the original critical incident. A common example is of women who are abused as children becoming prostitutes as young adults. These victims may be seeking some opportunity to reenact the original traumatic event to develop better mastery but a full explanation of this process is not known at this time.

Substance Abuse. A great many trauma victims self-medicate the symptoms of psychological trauma and PTSD to become calm, especially in the absence of other forms of treatment for trauma and PTSD.

Many victims have a drug of choice. If one knows the drug of choice, one knows the primary feeling state that the terrorist or traumatic event has left on the victim. This is called the self-medication hypothesis (Khantzian, 1997) and it is summarized in Table 3. Victims who are primarily using amphetamines and cocaine are self-medicating depression. Those using alcohol or barbiturates are self-medicating anxiety. Those who are using opiates are medicating anger and rage.

Table 3. Substance Use and the Self-medication Hypothesis

Substance	*Type of Psychological Distress*
Amphetamines Cocaine	Depression
Alcohol Barbiturates	Anxiety
Opiates	Anger

Risk Factors for PTSD

Not everyone who experiences a traumatic event goes on to develop PTSD. Research addressing this issue is ongoing, but some risk factors have been identified. About 30 percent of this propensity appears to be genetic (Almli, Fani, Smith & Ressler, 2014), but the specific genetic findings are not as yet clear. Further increasing the probability of developing PTSD are a dysfunctional family life in children, a previous trauma history, poor pre-incident coping skills, and a limited support network of caring attachments. Just as these caring attachments were important to the development of terrorists, they are equally important in victim recovery.

Treating Psychological Trauma and PTSD

Treating trauma victims is beyond the scope of this book. It is covered in detail elsewhere (Flannery, 2012a) and there are many therapists who specialize in treating trauma victims. The goal of this book is to alert readers who may have psychological trauma and PTSD to its presence in their lives and to encourage those who may be afflicted to seek help for recovery and a better quality of life.

The various treatments all address some common core issues. First, of course, is safety. No victim could begin to recover if the terrorists are still on the loose and pose a possible immediate, lingering threat. When reasonable safety has been restored, the next step in recovery is to address any self-medication issues that are of concern. Victims want to restore their brain and body chemistry to normal so that anxiety is reduced without the need to self-medicate.

A third recovery step is to reduce the unnecessary anxiety. There are at least three primary approaches that victims may choose from.

First is aerobic exercise. Brisk walking and other forms of exercise reduce stress quickly without the need for medicines. People with panic attacks should not choose this form of anxiety reduction, as aerobic exercise worsens panic attacks. A second form of managing anxiety is to talk to others about what has happened. This *ventilation,* as it is known, reduces the pressured feelings that can accompany terrorist events. People who are worriers in general will not find ventilation helpful, whereas aerobic exercise is usually a good fit for worriers. The third anxiety-reducing strategy is to map out a strategy in detail to recover from the terrorist event. This strategy is one of cognitive control and reduces stress by providing a sense of anticipated mastery.

A fourth recovery goal is to restore old or create new caring attachments. We have seen how good caring attachments provide both psychological and physiological benefits, the very resources that victims need in traumatic events. Real efforts should be expended to avoid withdrawal and self-isolation.

A fifth goal is to restore reasonable mastery, even if it is in just some small way. Since traumatic events destroy mastery, restoring one's mastery is an important component of recovery. Avoid decision avoidance. This occurs when victims want to put off until a later time the need to plan for recovery. Avoidance prolongs the suffering associated with psychological trauma.

The final goal is to restore a meaningful prosocial purpose in life so that living can again be seen as significant. To do this, however, brings us to the question with which we began this section of the book: Why me?

Why Me?

There are three components to restoring a meaningful prosocial purpose in life: grieving the loss, coming to grips with evil, and then putting one's suffering to some useful purpose. This resolves the question of why me.

All trauma involves loss as we have noted: life, liberty, property, mobility, and so forth. Victims no longer have an innocence about the world and realize, in a personal way, how cruel life and humans can be. The human response to loss is to grieve for what is gone. In this mourning process, victims need to review what was, what has been taken, and what life is like now after the terrorist event. Victims will likely feel anger, anxiety, sadness, guilt, and/or depression. Victims should do this review in small, gradual steps, and repeat the review process until the victim is at peace with it.

Terrorism and other forms of human-perpetrated violence are evil. They destroy the inherent goodness of the created universe. The question *Why me?* reflects the victim's awareness that this event is not right, is not fair, and that as good people they have done nothing to warrant this. They were the wrong people in the wrong places at the wrong times. Terrorists attack innocent civilians to produce exactly this state of distress and disorientation. Victims have encountered evil and need to understand what it is. Ministers of the various faith traditions can be of great help in these matters.

There are some basic understandings of evil. One school posits that good and bad are part of the created universe and must be accepted. A second approach is that every person has a basic right to justice, love, and respect, and that to violate the basic rights of anyone is evil. Still other faith traditions see human beings as agents of free choice who can follow the basic principles of goodness in the created universe or can choose to destroy that basic goodness. Based on their values and beliefs, victims need to choose whatever system is most helpful in understanding why what has happened took place.

With the losses grieved and an understanding of evil in place, the last step in recovering meaning is to put one's suffering in the service of others. Mothers Against Drunk Driving (MADD) is a good example of people who have put their personal suffering into a cause to prevent other families from having to go through the same ordeal. If the original meaningful purpose is life entailed helping others, this original purpose can be thus restored and provide a meaningful transition through the terrorist incident. Others may find that as they restore their original meaningful purpose, it may now be shaped somewhat to include others in a new way.

Why me? becomes *How can I help others?*

TERRORISM: RISK MANAGEMENT STRATEGIES

PART 4

Terrorism:
Risk Management Strategies

Truth crushed to the earth will rise again.
—William Jennings Bryan

Nothing is so much to be feared as fear.
—Henry David Thoreau

Dateline: Mumbai, India, November 26, 2008
The Taj Mahal Palace Hotel, the Grande Dame of Mumbai, is famous for its central floating staircase, 1,500 staff that includes 35 butlers, several elegant bars and restaurants. Certainly it was a palace and perfect blueprint for a comfortable stay. They settled in.

Even as they settled in, a boat was being commandeered at sea by ten terrorists. They then made their way to the Mumbai shore and proceeded to attack several city sites in teams of two.

At 9:45 P.M., the terrorists stormed the Taj Mahal Hotel, attacking guests at random by the swimming pool. They then moved to the lobby and restaurants. There were massive explosions: one in the lobby, two in elevators, and three in the restaurants. The terrorists went from floor to floor seeking out targets. They lit fires and threw grenades as they went. At 3 A.M., the building was on fire.

The stench of death was everywhere. Guests blown apart in the explosions, Guests shot at point-blank range. Guests who had suffocated in the smoke. The firefighters were heroic in their efforts to save guests.

The terrorists were ten men who were handpicked from a group of twenty-four. They had received training in basic combat, high-end weapons and explosives, as well as marine warfare. The assailants used satellite and cell phones to speak to each other and then their handlers in Pakistan. The basic plan of attack went smoothly as they had expected. They had blueprints for each site, including the floor plan of the Taj Mahal hotel.

It was a perfect blueprint for murder. As is the pattern, nothing was left to chance.

Here is another vivid example of the carnage that terrorist incidents create. We have spent considerable time examining and understanding terrorism, the assailants who do these things, the weapons of destruction at their disposal, and the impact of these events on civilian victims. This enriched understanding has taught us who terrorists are and what they are about. This knowledge also begins to give us some control of the situation and to reduce our anxiety. This understanding further gives rise to risk management strategies to prevent and disrupt terrorist activity and to cope effectively and quickly in those instances wherein terrorist violence does occur. It is this information which is the focus of this last part of the book.

No one can predict violence with one-hundred percent accuracy, as we have noted. However, good risk management strategies can seriously reduce the risk of violence and enhance the safety of civilians. Good risk management strategies employ the same four-stage model that terrorists use to carry out attacks (See Table 3 in part 1, page 31) in order to disrupt or minimize those very attacks before they can take place: selecting the target, pre-event planning, the counterinsurgency event execution, and post-incident analysis to improve the safety of a country's citizens. Risk management strategies are interventions designed to prevent, disrupt, and/or reduce the impact of any terrorist event. Risk management strategies are also designed to destroy the terrorist enemy over time—leader by leader, group by group, weapon by weapon, dollar by dollar. Terrorist events are complex in nature, so the dismantling process takes time but each counterinsurgent attack weakens the enemy and increases the safety of the nation's victim citizens. Understanding terrorism is important because it provides needed information to create risk management strategies specifically tapered to the enemy that result in the disruption of terrorist events. Both understanding and an awareness of sound counterinsurgent risk management strategies together should assure the citizens of the country that they are safe, protected on an ongoing basis, and that normal daily life can continue.

Finally, we have spoken about the importance of reasonable mastery, a network of caring attachments, and a meaningful prosocial purpose in life as the fundamentals of good physical and mental health. We have seen how these domains become disrupted, although for different reasons, in both assailants and victims. We civilians also want to have these skills in our own lives so that in an age of terrorism, we correctly feel in control, can interact with our friends and neighbors, can lead meaningful lives, and not be unduly worried and anxious about terrorist events. Understanding the enemy can result in some reduction in anxiety as citizens learn what they are factually up against. Risk management strategies by one's country and basic stress management skills for citizens can complete the process of taking control and moving on safely in one's life.

Using the United States government as a model for counterinsurgency, we turn first to the various risk management strategies that the government has put in place, which greatly enhances our day-to-day safety and requires no action on our part. Then, we shall examine various strategies that individuals can employ to manage the stress of living in this age of terrorism. These individual stress management skills can also be helpful in other issues in life that can increase anxiety from time to time. Our goal is to have reasonable mastery, a network of caring attachments, and a meaningful purpose in our lives.

Risk Management Strategies for Safety

Although differing countries may understandably choose to emphasize, add, or disregard certain counterinsurgency strategies as befits their specific needs, in the United States various levels of government provide a triple-layer of risk management strategies to protect its citizens. In dealing with terrorists, there are two fundamental approaches: utilize diplomacy to see if some reasonable resolution may be attained and/or wage intense military warfare to defeat the enemy directly. The United States utilizes both approaches simultaneously.

The Federal Government

The first responsibility of any government is to protect its citizens and terrorism is not an exception to this rule. How best to do this is more complicated in the U.S., since it is a democracy and must find a balance between strategies to protect its people, while at the same time honoring their basic civil rights.

Diplomacy. In its war against terrorism, the U.S. has often employed diplomacy to see if there are ways to stop or prevent warfare. This includes meeting with terrorist representatives or other nation–states representing the terrorists' interests to see if the alleged grievance in any given terrorist group's cause can be addressed in nonviolent ways. From time to time, these efforts have included humanitarian and various forms of economic aid. Public education about possible solutions has also been fielded to educate the civilian populace of the enemy to help them under-stand possible solutions to the conflict other than armed war-fare. Sometimes this has been attempted by dropping leaflets; at other times the various forms of media, including social media, have been utilized. The federal government also fields the Voice of America and Alhurra, an Arabic language television station to inform listeners of United States values and policies.

Military Intervention. Certainly, fielding and maintaining a standing army is a crucial message to potential enemies that attacking the country will bring serious, if not permanent failure. Civilians are usually aware of the military's known fighting capac-ity. In the hunt to root out terrorists, the use of Special Forces, bombings by aircraft and drones, and the training of allied forces in terrorist territory have become helpful strategies in killing terrorist leaders and group combatants and in degrading and destroying their weaponry. While fielding of entire military brigades is usually not necessary to defeat circumscribed terrorist enclaves, the military force of the United States stands second to none in the world.

Military Intelligence. However, military interventions involve more than actual physical combat. A large part of the military's efforts involve intelligence gathering through espionage, agents in the enemy's area of operation, paid informers, and in our technological age increasing assessment of electronic surveillance. This electronic surveillance is known as SIGNIT (signals intelligence) and includes telephone calls, faxes, radio signals, and information on the internet. The federal government gathers this information in multiple languages and employs several translators, cryptologists, and data analysts to assess the information gathered. Sometime, the intelligence yields more information than human-gathered information from the field. The United States partners with Australia, Canada, New Zealand, and the United Kingdom in the gathering and sharing of intelligence. This worldwide intelligence network gathers information on an ongoing basis on terrorist plans, finances, training, and travel plans (Hayden, 2016). The United States has also created an electronic computer weapon, Stuxnet, that can disrupt enemy financing, power, lighting, and the like.

We saw in the vignette opening this part how the terrorists in the field in India were communicating with their group leaders in Pakistan who were watching events unfold in real time and were sending directives to their terrorist colleagues in the field. This demonstrates the power of gathering and utilizing electronic intelligence as a potential deterrent but intelligence becomes a delicate balancing act in a democracy wherein individual citizens have a right to privacy. This issue may emerge in the gathering of intelligence through interrogation and detention policies, especially in the cases of lone wolves who may be citizens. Citizens should remember that the government is gathering intelligence and then, based on this intelligence tapering military interventions on an ongoing basis, twenty-four/seven, to ensure citizen safety.

Homeland Security. In addition to the military preparedness and intelligence gathering noted above, the United States government created an overarching security agency in the aftermath of the 9/11 attacks in New York City. This agency, known as Homeland Security, is charged with protecting the citizenry and the infrastructure needed for daily life from external/internal threats and aggressive acts. While most citizens are aware of Homeland Security through their air travels, the agency's mission is much broader and includes aviation, border, port, cyber, and chemical security as well as response preparedness for terrorist events and manmade or natural disasters. Some but not all of the participating agencies include the Emergency Management Agency, the Coast Guard, Customs and Immigration, the Federal Bureau of Investigation, and the Secret Service, and provide some sense of the extent and thoroughness of protecting the citizenry.

Toward this end, the federal government fields a variety of specific interventions to secure citizen safety by making attacks more difficult to carry out due to this added security. These strategies may include deploying more personnel to high-risk areas, such as airports, mass-transit systems, power plants, and large political, cultural, or athletic events.

In addition to protecting its people, Homeland Security is also responsible for securing the country's infrastructure. This includes hardening more common possible targets such as government buildings, schools, power plants, etc. by utilizing crime prevention through environmental design (CPTED; Crowe, 1991). CPTED works on the basic principle that one can reduce the risk of violence by designing the environment to thwart typical terrorist and criminal strategies. For example, placing shrubs around an agency that are low in size and physically away from the building itself to thwart a terrorist from hiding behind the shrubbery and then robbing, raping, or kidnapping some targeted person deemed essential. Some common examples include governmental agencies improving security access by adding traffic barriers in front of important civil and government buildings. Again, these and similar interventions enhance citizen safety and protect needed infrastructure to ensure ongoing daily life with minimal disruptions.

Health Care. Another important area for federal government intervention is ensuring that people will be safe and medically cared for in the event of a terrorist attack, be it conventional bombing or the release of deadly toxins in a WMD event.

As a first step, the government addresses what is known as surge capacity. Surge capacity refers to an expected increase in the number of injured civilians in the aftermath of an attack. These plans include being sure that there are enough hospital beds, that enough doctors who can be summoned quickly, that there are enough medicines to meet the need, and that there is an ambulance or transportation system that is geared up for the need. Much of the work that is needed in a disaster falls to the Red Cross, and that is discussed separately below.

The broad array of federal government programs in direct military contact, intelligence and communication gathering, the role of Homeland Security, the basic forms of target hardening, and the efforts already in place to save lives and hasten recovery in the event of a terrorist incident should bring a sense of reasonable safety and security.

We turn next to additional measures for civilian safety and security found at the state and local levels.

State and Local Government

State and local governments provide two additional levels of protection against possible terrorists, again with no required effort from the average citizen.

Again using the United States as a paradigm model, the U.S. Constitution gives the states' National Guards the authority to protect the homeland. They are local citizens, know the local terrain, and train locally. Since they are located nearby, they provide an immediate response capacity.

While National Guard units are at times sent overseas for military service, most of their efforts are applied in the homeland. Their training includes combat readiness in a variety of settings as well as response to national and manmade disasters. They often supplement manpower in response to federal government requests, and they are in continuous contact with the national and local intelligence-gathering sources. Since they know the local terrain, they can strengthen target-hardening efforts for possible local targets needed for daily living such as power plants, highways, and other forms of needed transportation, hospitals, and similar basic components necessary to keep the community functioning. They work closely with the state and local policing authorities to maintain constant vigilance.

National Guard units also play a critical role in responding to manmade and natural disasters. They work in concert with the national and local Red Cross units, save lives, and work to restore normal community functioning as quickly as possible. Again, the response to disasters will be considered separately, shortly.

We think of men and women in the National Guard as weekend warriors in the local armory. In truth, they are an additional source of safety and security for civilians and may play an important role in preventing, disrupting, and assisting in the recovery from terrorist incidents.

Crisis Response. Should the worst happen and the rare terrorist event take place, civilians would be understandably frightened but should take comfort in knowing that the federal, state, and local governments have spent many hours in training, learning how best to respond and to restore normal community life as quickly as possible.

Disasters are overwhelming events that test the adaptive responses of communities and/or individuals beyond their normal capabilities and result in massive disruptions to daily functioning (Raphael, 1986). Large-scale terrorist events like those examples noted at the beginning of each part count as disasters. Any affected community or group of civilians must respond to four basic tasks: safety and survival, resources to rebuild, restore social networks, and restore normal daily living as quickly as possible. The Red Cross is usually the lead agent in these events.

The Red Cross sets up an incident-command center and begins by marshaling police, fire, National Guard, and/or paramedics to triage the wounded and to see to it that they are transferred to the nearest hospital, a hospital that has already been put on alert to expect victims. The deceased victims are removed from the site.

With this first step in place, the Red Cross at the federal, state, and local levels begin to address an array of tasks and services that are crucial for victims of a terrorist event to begin to restore some semblance of daily functioning and community. Arrangements are made for mass care, which includes the provisions of shelter, feeding, and medical care for every civilian affected by the event and in need of such services. The Red Cross also assumes responsibility for managing any shelter that it provides, so that civilians will be safe and secure.

At the same time, it begins a block-by-block damage assessment of the impacted area to see what public-health services (e.g., water, sewer, electric grid) are functioning and what homes are safe to occupy. This information is electronically stored for property owners and the federal housing agencies to access in terms of insurance claims and mobilizing any needed resources. These resources may vary greatly from ice, plywood, fencing, and telephone poles to hiring emergency construction workers and contacting undertakers.

A third major effort is to begin to restore, enhance, or create anew a meaningful social support network for people, animals, and pets. Each shelter keeps an inventory of those present, and continuous efforts are made to link up family units. Assistance is requested from and provided by the religious leaders of the basic faith traditions, so that small neighborhood groupings in shelters can begin to come together.

A last major task for the Red Cross is to provide crisis counseling services for those in need. The federal government utilizes a program called psychological first aid in which local citizens are trained in advance to provide basic crisis services in times of disaster. States have their own crisis counseling teams to be fielded. These are often located in the states' department of emergency services or department of mental health. The American Psychological Association has fielded a team of trained psychologists to provide additional counseling services in all fifty states. My own crisis counseling service, the Assaulted Staff Action Program (*ASAP,* Flannery, 2012), originally designed for staff victims of patient assaults, is responsive to the needs of all victims of psychological trauma, and has been utilized by a local Red Cross chapter. Any victim found to have more intense psychological needs in any of these acute crisis counseling services is then referred on for individual or group counseling.

These crisis counseling services are usually mandated for the first-responder community that is seeking to restore normalcy for their fellow citizens as quickly as possible. First responders are often traumatized by their encounters with death, especially relatives, neighbors, or children; the anguish and suffering of survivors; and the physical dangers that may be encountered in fires, burning chemicals, and emitted toxins. Often, civilians do not realize that the first-responder community has more cases of PTSD than returning military victims. Hence, the need for crisis counseling services for them as well.

All of these disaster relief services by all levels of government are meant to restore normal community life as quickly as possible, so that citizens' having to camp out is kept to the barest minimum. Large numbers of our fellow citizens spend countless hours in pre-incident trainings to be able to provide these services to fellow citizens in terms of emergency and after, even when their own personal and family lives have been disrupted by the same terrorist incident.

* * *

We have seen how enhanced understanding of terrorism can began to reduce our anxiety about such matters because this knowledge has resulted in a vast array of risk management strategies to prevent and/or disrupt these terrorist forays and how to cope effectively, immediately, and efficiently to those few incidents that may occur. These federal, state, and local initiatives permit their citizens to feel in control and to lead normal lives. See the summary in Table 1.

It is true, however, that we do live in an age of terrorism as well as one of rapid modernization and globalization. These and

Table 1. Governmental Risk Management Strategies

Federal Government
    Diplomacy
    Combat Readiness
    Intelligence Gathering/Communications
    Homeland Security
    Health-Care Surge Planning
State and Local Government
    National Guard
    Information Gathering/Communications
    Target Hardening
    Federal, State, and Local Governments
    Disaster Relief

the normal stressful life events that we all encounter can be further addressed by stress management strategies that individuals can adopt and adapt in their own lives. I have written about these matters at length (Flannery, 2012d). A brief overview is presented here but can be studied in more depth in the work cited. The interventions noted in this review enhance mastery, caring attachments, and a meaningful prosocial purpose in life, and result in reduced anxiety and improved health.

Right Brain Activities. The cortex is that part of the brain where we do our problem solving and select how we will respond. In general, the left cortex of the brain is for language, thinking, and problem solving. The right cortex is for visual–spatial locomotion in the environment so that we can move about without hurting ourselves. Both of these spheres of the brain cannot be equally active at the same time. One is always more active than the other side. Worrying and its accompanying anxiety begin in the left brain. But Nature has a secret. If one activates the right brain, it will dampen the worry in the left brain. The more one uses right-brain activities the less stress one has. Some common right-brain activities include aerobic exercising, brisk walking, relaxation exercises, yoga, biofeedback, prayer, humor, art, music, and dance. The good thing about using right-brain activities to reduce stress is that your brain will not allow you to do this in the face of an actual life-threatening event.

Wise Lifestyle Choices. There are some basic health practices that have been shown to result in good health and a sense of well-being. These include no smoking, regular sleep patterns, regular meals/no snacks with an emphasis on a plant-based diet, breakfast every day, moderate or no drinking, maintaining normal body weight, and regular exercise. These lifestyle choices can be implemented in your life over a period of six months to two years at no cost to you.

Stress-resistant Persons. For over twelve years, I followed twelve-hundred people to see who coped well with stress and what their successful strategies were (Flannery, 2012c). Table 2 presents a summary of the six characteristics that emerged.

The first skill was reasonable mastery. As we saw earlier, the adaptive copers correctly identify the problems before them, gather information to solve the problems, implement some possible solutions, and check to see whether they had worked. They were aware that at times they did not have the resources to solve the problems and brought in some forms of extra help or moved on in life.

Table 2. Stress-resistant Persons

---

1. Reasonable Mastery
2. Personal Commitment to a Task

Wise Lifestyle Choices

- Few Dietary Stimulants
- Aerobic Exercise
- Relaxation Exercise

3. Social Supports
4. Sense of Humor
5. Concern for Welfare of Others

Stress-resistant persons all had some task in life that was important to them. Getting a promotion at work, enhancing the quality of their relationships, rearing children, a special community project are common examples. Stress-resistant persons also make wise lifestyle choices such as avoiding the dietary stimulants of caffeine and refined white sugar, (stimulants that will increase anxiety), engaging in aerobic exercises, and having a period of relaxation every day. They also maintain good social supports, call upon their sense of humor, and are concerned for the welfare of others in a great variety of ways.

Stress-resistant persons used the first, third, and fifth characteristics in Table 2 to enhance mastery. They utilize characteristics two, four, and six to enhance caring attachments and to develop prosocial, meaningful purposes in life.

In terms of terrorist events specifically, stress-resistant persons stay sober; pay attention to their surroundings; avoid large crowds; move away from airport-security areas quickly in air terminals; and know to say something, if they see something.

* * *

We have now completed our concise overview of terrorism and the many multiple layers of risk management strategies put in place to allow us to lead our lives freely without undue concern. These various government safety procedures and any of our individual stress management skills really do leave us in control. We do not have undue fears of car accidents and being struck by lightning. We act accordingly at the time and then continue on with our lives. Dealing with terrorist threats need not be different.

References and Select Readings

Almli, L. M., Favi, N., Smith, A. K., and Ressler, K. J. (2014). Genetic approaches to understanding post-traumatic stress disorder. *International Journal of Neuropsychopharmacology, 17,* 355–70.

American Psychiatric Association (eds.) (2013). *Diagnostic and Statistical Manual of Mental Disorders.* Fifth Edition. Washington, DC: American Psychiatric Press.

Antonovsky, A. (1979). *Health, Stress, and Coping.* San Francisco: Jossey–Bass.

Blanco, A, Blanco, R, and Diaz, D. (2016). Social (dis)order and psychological trauma: Look earlier, look outside, and look beyond the persons. *American Psychologist,* 71, 187–98.

Bowlby, J. (1982). *Attachment and Loss, vol. 1: Attachment.* Second edition. New York: Basic Books.

Carr, C. (2002). *The Lessons of Terror: A History of Warfare against Civilians: Why It Has Failed and Why It Will Again.* New York: Random House.

Cronin, I., (ed.) (2002). *Confronting Fear: A History of Terrorism.* New York: Basic Books.

Crowe, T. D. (1991). *Crime Prevention through Environmental Design: Application of Architectural Design and Space Management Concepts.* Stoneham, MA: Butterworth–Heineman.

Davis, P., and Jenkins, B. M. (2002). *Deterrence and Influences in Counterterrorism: A Component on the War on Al-Queda.* Santa Monica, CA: Rand.

Deikman, A. J. (2003). *Them and Us: Cult Thinking and Terrorist Threat.* Berkeley, CA: Bay Tree.

Durant, W., and Durant, A. (1968). *The Lessons of History.* New York: Simon and Schuster.

Durkheim, É. (1997). *Suicide: A study in Sociology.* Trans: Spaulding, J. and Simpson, G. New York: Free Press.

Dutton, D. (2007). *The Psychology of Genocide, Massacres, and Extreme Violence: Why "Normal" People Come to Commit Atrocities.* Westport, CT: Praeger Security International.

Flannery, R. B. Jr. (2009). *The Violent Person: Professional Risk Management Strategies for Safety and Care.* Riverdale, NY: American Mental Health Foundation.

———. (2012a). *Posttraumatic Stress Disorder: The Victim's Guide to Healing and Recovery.* Riverdale, NY: American Mental Health Foundation.

———. (2012b). *The Assaulted Staff Action Program (ASAP): Coping with the Psychological Aftermath of Violence.* Riverdale, NY: American Mental Health Foundation.

———. (2012c). *Becoming Stress-Resistant through the Project SMART Program.* Riverdale, NY: American Mental Health Foundation.

————. (2016). *Violence: Why People Do Bad Things with Strategies to Reduce that Risk.* Riverdale, NY: American Mental Health Foundation.

Forest, J. (2015). *The Terrorism Lectures.* Second edition, Santa Ana, CA: Norita Press.

Friedman, L. S. (ed.) (2004). *What Motivates Suicide Bombers?* Oxford, UK: Oxford University Press.

Hayden, M. (2016). *Playing to the Edge: American Intelligence in an Age of Terror.* New York: Penguin.

Hoffer, E. (1966). *The True Believer.* New York: Harper and Row.

Horgan, J. (2014). *The Psychology of Terrorism.* Second edition. New York: Routledge.

Howitt, A. M., and Pang, R. L. (eds.) (2003). *Countering Terrorism: Dimensions of Preparedness.* Cambridge, MA: MIT Press.

Ignafieff, M. (2004). *The Lesser Evil: Political Politics in an Age of Terror.* Princeton, NJ: Princeton University Press.

Kayyem, J. N., and Pangi, R. (eds.) (2003). *First to Arrive: State and Local Response to Terrorism.* Cambridge, MA: MIT Press.

Khantzian, E. J. (1997). The self-medication hypothesis of substance use disorders: A reconsideration of recent applications. *Harvard Review of Psychiatry,* 4, 231–44.

Laquer, W. (1999). *The New Face of Terrorism: Fanaticism and the Arms of Mass Destruction.* New York: Oxford University Press.

———. (2003). *No End to War: Terrorism in the Twenty-first Century.* New York: Continuum International.

Litz, B. (Ed.) (2004). *Early Interventions for Trauma and Traumatic Loss.* New York: Guilford.

Lynch, J. (1977). *The Broken Heart: The Medical Consequences of Loneliness.* New York: Basic Books.

———. (2000). *A Cry Unheard: New Insights into the Medical Consequences of Loneliness.* Baltimore: Bancroft Press.

Mailman School of Public Health (2015). PTSD and depression in survivors a decade after 9/11. *Chronic Disease,* Jan. 9.

Minter, R. (2004). *The Shadow War: The Untold Story of How America Is Winning the War of Terrorism.* Washington, DC: Regency.

Moghaddam, F., and Marsella, A. J. (eds.) (2004). *Understanding Terrorism: Psychosocial Roots, Consequences, and Interventions.* Washington, DC: American Psychological Association.

Napoleoni, L. (2003). *Modern Jihad: Tracing the Dollars behind the Terror Networks.* London: Pluto.

Norrholm, S. D., and Ressler, K. J. (2009). Genetics of anxiety and trauma-related disorders. *Neuroscience,* 164, 273–87. New York: HarperCollins.

Pape, R.A. (2005). *Dying to Win: The Strategic Logic of Suicide Terrorism.* New York: Random House.

Raphael, B. (1986). *When Disaster Strikes: How Individuals and Communities Cope.* New York: Basic Books.

Simon, T.D. (2013). *Lone wolf terrorism: Understanding the growing threat.* Amherst, NY: Prometheus.

Stout, C. E. (ed.). (2002). *Psychology of Terrorism, vol 4: Programs and Practices in Response and Prevention.* Westport, CT: Praeger.

Terkel, S. (2003). *Hope Dies Last: Keeping Faith in Difficult Times.* New York: Free Press.

Traverso, E. (2003). *The Origins of Nazi Violence.* New York: Free Press.

About the Author

Raymond B. Flannery Jr., Ph.D., FAPM, is a licensed clinical psychologist and fellow of the Academy of Psychosomatic Medicine. He is Associate Professor of Psychology, Department of Psychiatry (Part-Time), Harvard Medical School, and Adjunct Assistant Professor of Psychiatry, Department of Psychiatry, The University of Massachusetts Medical School.

For 10 years, Dr. Flannery was Director of Training for the Massachusetts Department of Mental Health. He has lectured extensively throughout North America and Europe. He is the author of 9 books, and of more than 165 peer-reviewed articles in the medical and scientific journals on topics of stress, violence, and victimization. His work has been translated into 5 languages.

Dr. Flannery designed and fielded the Assaulted Staff Action Program (ASAP), a voluntary, peer-help, crisis-intervention program for employee victims of violence. For more than a quarter-century, he has overseen the development of this program, now including 2,200 ASAP team members on 45 teams in 9 states that have responded to the needs of over 9,000 staff victims. ASAP is the most widely researched crisis-intervention program in the

world, and has been chosen as a best innovative practice intervention by the federal governments of the United States and Canada.
Dr. Flannery also designed and directed the longest continuous
study of assaultive psychiatric patients in the published literature.

In 2005, Dr. Flannery received a lifetime achievement award
for excellence in crisis-intervention research from the International Critical Incident Stress Foundation.